RECORDED VERSIONS
GUITAR

AUTHENTIC TRANSCRIPTIONS
WITH NOTES AND TABLATURE

B.B. KING
LIVE AT THE REGAL

Music transcriptions by Pete Billmann, Aurelien Budynek and Martin Shellard

ISBN 978-1-4803-9620-3

HAL•LEONARD®
CORPORATION

7777 W. BLUEMOUND RD. P.O. BOX 13819 MILWAUKEE, WI 53213

Visit Hal Leonard Online at
www.halleonard.com

Every Day I Have the Blues

Words and Music by Peter Chatman

*Chord symbols reflect basic harmony.

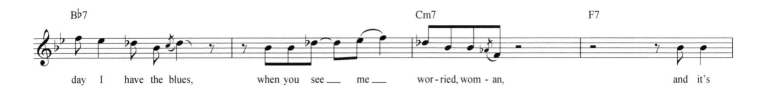

day I have the blues, when you see ___ me ___ wor-ried, wom-an, and it's

Verse

you I hate ___ to lose. 2. No-bod-y loves me, ___ no-bod-y seem to

care. Yes, no-bod-y loves me, no-bod-y seem to

care, ___ speak-ing of wor-ries and trou - ble, dar-lin', you know ___ I've had my share.

Guitar Solo

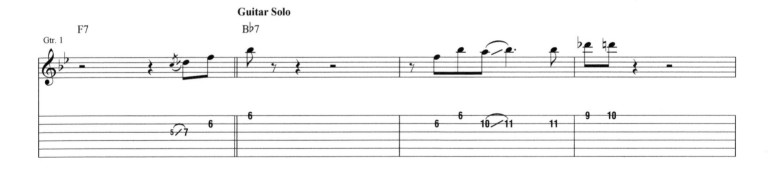

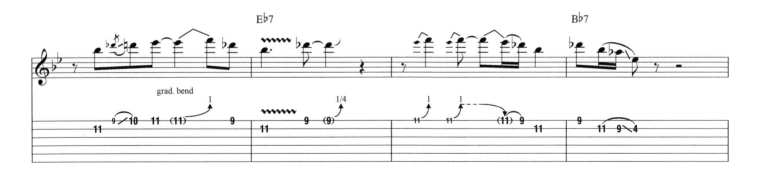

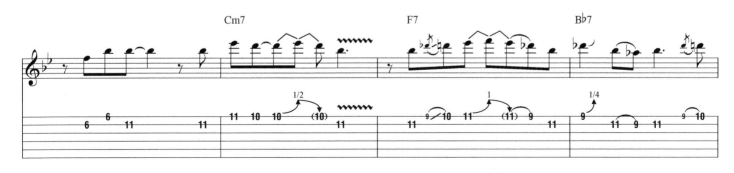

*Switch to bridge pickup.

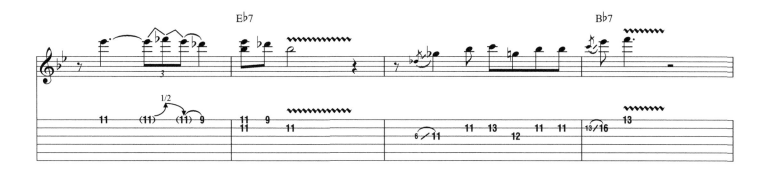

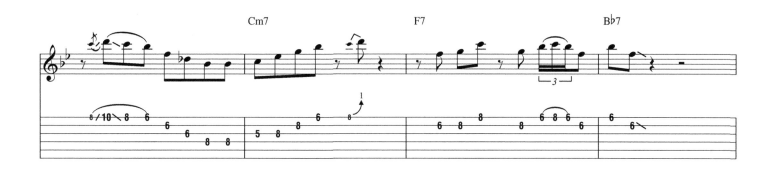

Verse

Gtr. 1 tacet

3. Ev - 'ry day, ev - 'ry day, ev - 'ry day, ev - 'ry

day, __ ev - 'ry __ day, __ ev - 'ry day I have the blues, __

__ when you see __ me wor - ried, wom - an, and it's you I hate __ to lose.

Verse

F7   Bb7

4. Ev - 'ry day, _____ ev - 'ry day ____ I have the blues, ____

Eb7   Bb7

____ ev - 'ry ____ day, ____ ev - 'ry day I have the blues, ____

Cm7   F7

____ when you see ____ me wor - ried, wom - an, yes, it's ____

Bb7   B7 Bb7

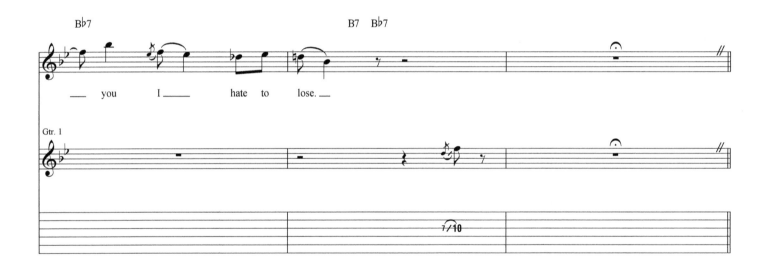

____ you I ____ hate to lose. ____

Gtr. 1

7/10

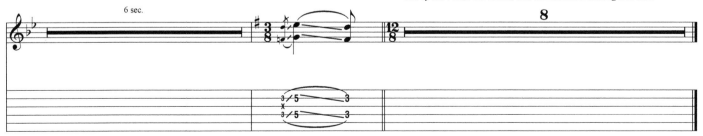

Interlude
Free time

Spoken: Thank you, thank you, thank you very much.

Slower ♩ = 61

Outro

*Spoken: Thank you so much, and now, ladies and gentlemen, we would
like to go back and sort of reminisce just a little bit, and pick up
some of the real old blues. If we should happen to play one that
you remember, let us know it by making some noise, if we should
pick up one that you might remember. We'd like to start it off by
one of the real, real oldies, and it sounds something like this.*

6 sec.

Sweet Little Angel

Words and Music by B.B. King and Jules Bihari

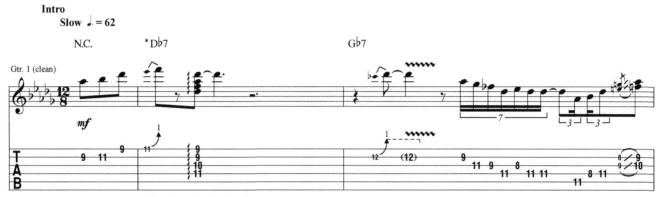

*Chord symbols reflect basic harmony.

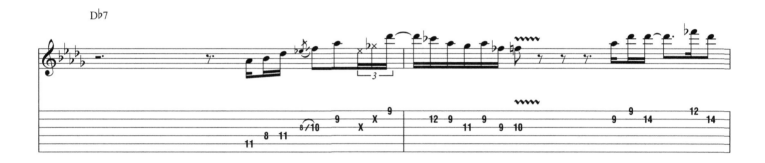

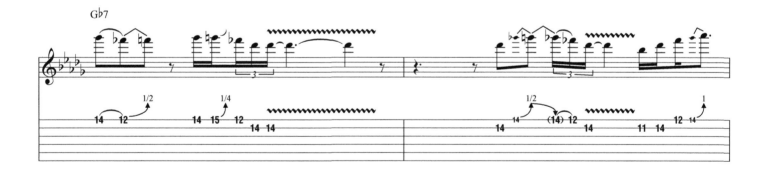

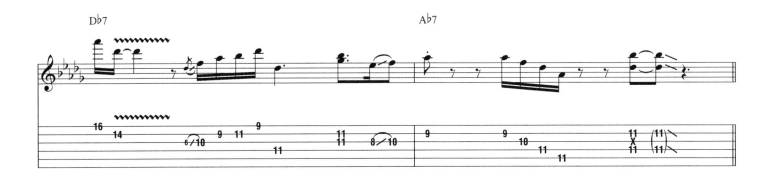

Verse

Gtr. 1 tacet

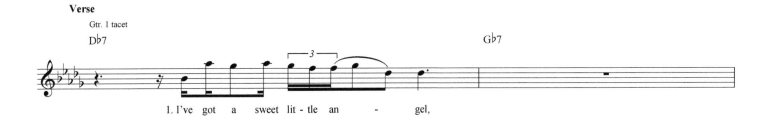

1. I've got a sweet lit - tle an - gel,

I love ___ the way _____ she spread her wings. Yes, got

a sweet lit - tle an - gel, I love ___ the way _____

_____ she spread her ___ wings. _____ Yes, ___ when she spread ___

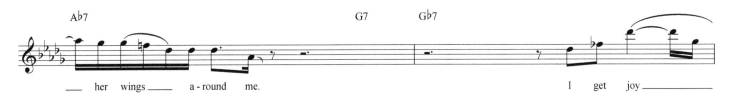

___ her wings ___ a - round me. I get joy _____

and ev-'ry-thing.

Verse

2. You know, I asked my ba-by for a nick-el, and she gave

me a twen-ty dol-lar bill. Oh, yes,

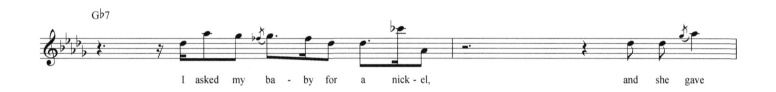

I asked my ba-by for a nick-el, and she gave

me a twen-ty dol-lar bill. Whooh, ya know, I ask her for

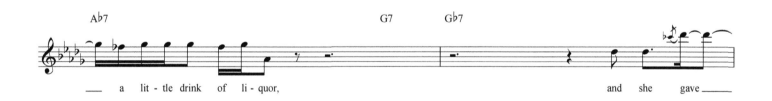

a lit-tle drink of li-quor, and she gave

me a whis-ky still. 3. Oh, if

Verse

my ba - by should quit me, Lord I do be-lieve

I would die. _____ Oh, _____ if _____

my ba - by _____ should quit me, _____ Lord I ____ do be - lieve ____

I would die. _____ Yes, __ if you don't love __

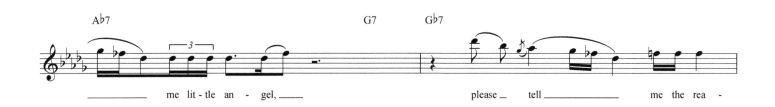

_____ me lit - tle an - gel, _____ please ___ tell _____ me the rea -

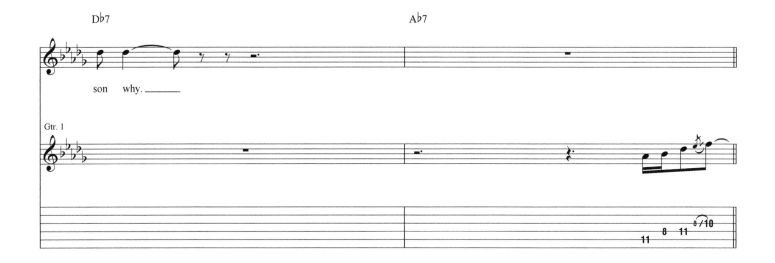

son why. _____

Gtr. 1

Guitar Solo

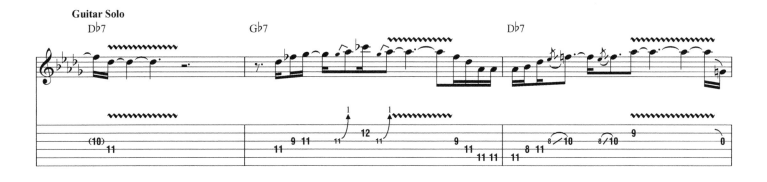

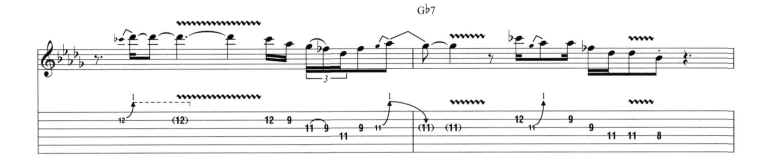

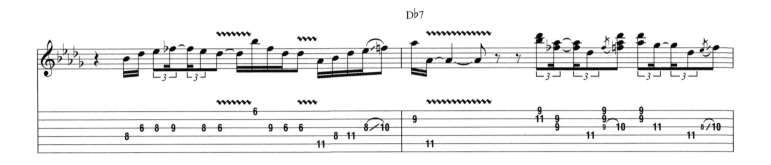

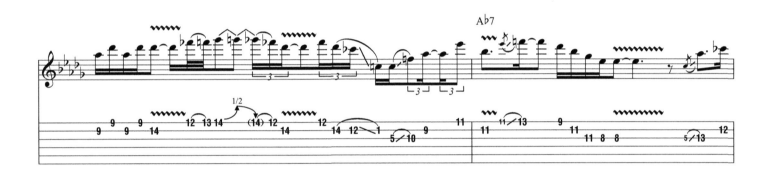

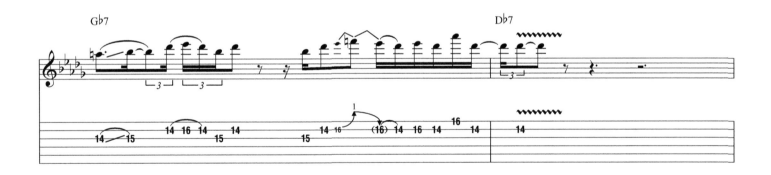

Outro

Spoken: Thank you, well, I hope you remember that one.

Thank you. I'd like to tell you a little story now, if I may. A guy singing about his girlfriend and he calls her his "angel", of course that's the "sweet little angel", but let's think about a guy that loses his girl. Oh, it happens, believe me. And then he starts to sing...

Gtr. 1 tacet

Ab7

8

It's My Own Fault Darlin'

Words and Music by B.B. King and Jules Bihari

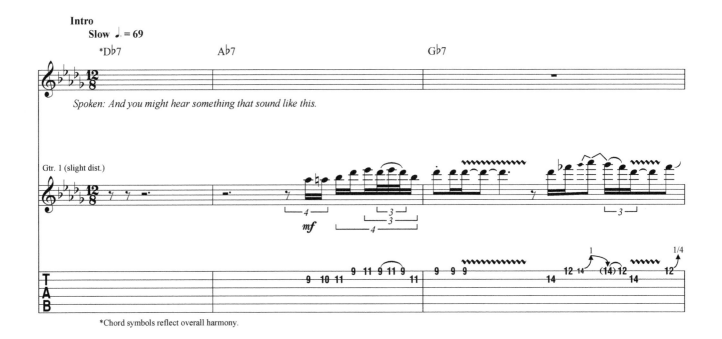

Spoken: And you might hear something that sound like this.

*Chord symbols reflect overall harmony.

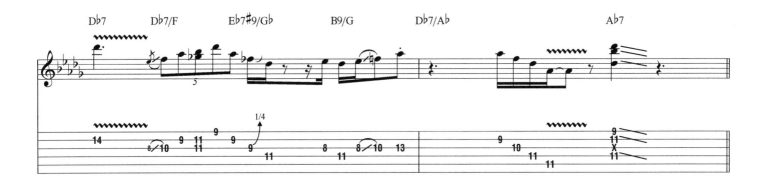

Verse

Gtr. 1 tacet

1. It's my own ___ fault, ___ babe, ___   treat me the way ___ you wan-na do.

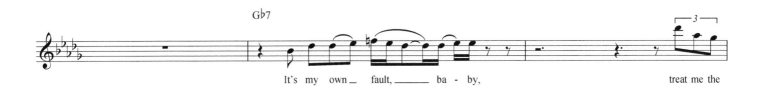

It's my own ___ fault, ___ ba-by,   treat me the

way _____ you wan-na do.   Yes, _ when you were lov - ing _ me, _ ba - by,

Oh, ____ at that time _____ lit-tle girl ____ I did-n't love you.   This is the part I

Verse

like.   2. She used to make her own pay checks   and bring them on home ___

___ to me.   I would go out on the hill - side you know and make   ev - 'ry ___ wo - man drunk ___

___ I see. ___ And it's my own _ fault, _ ba - by.   Treat me the way _____ you wan-na do.

Oh, ___ yes, ___ when you were lov - ing me, wo - man.   Oh, ___ at ___

that _ time, _____ lit - tle girl, _____ I did-n't love __ you. *Spoken: I have one more I wanna tell you.*

Verse

3. She said she was gon-na leave __ me. She'd been run-ning a-round with the boys. __

She said she was gon-na __ leave _____ me, gon - na be o - ver Il - li - nois. __

And it's my own __ fault, __ ba - by. Treat me the way _____ you wan-na do.

Oh, _____ when you were lov - ing me, wo-man. Oh, _____ at that __

__ time, _____ lit - tle girl, _____ I did-n't love you. What you say? All right!

Gtr. 1

Outro-Guitar Solo

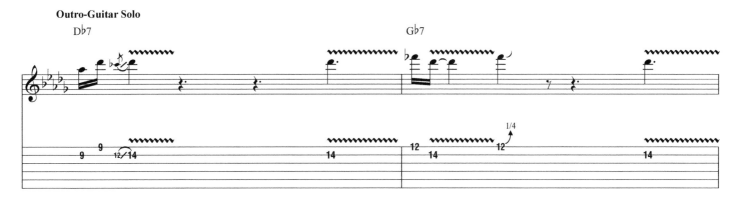

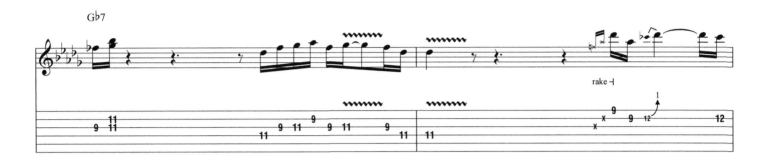

Segue to "How Blue Can You Get"

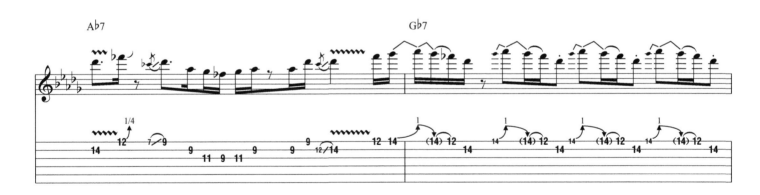

How Blue Can You Get

By Leonard Feather

*Chord symbols reflect overall harmony.

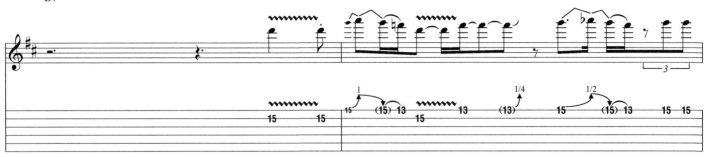

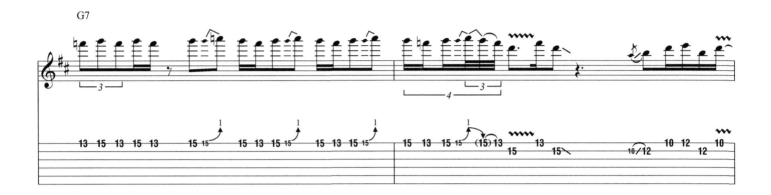

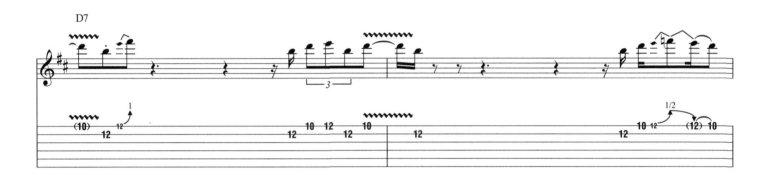

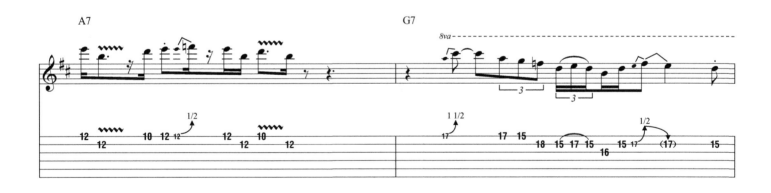

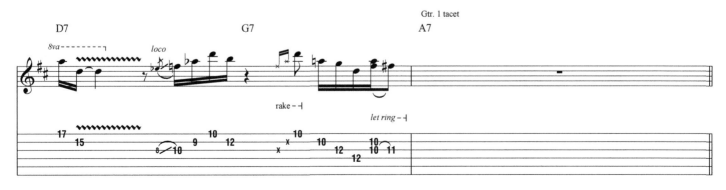

Verse

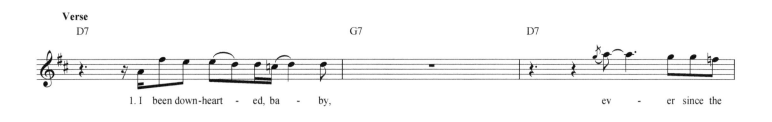

1. I been down-heart - ed, ba - by, ev - er since the

day we met. I say, I've been down heart - ed, ba - by,

ev - er since the day we met. Ah, but love is noth-ing but the blues,

wo - man. Ba - by, how blue can you get?

Verse

2. You're e - vil when I'm with you, and you are jeal - ous when we're a - part.

Yes, I say, you're e - vil, you're so e - vil when I'm with you, ba -

- by. And you are jeal-ous when we're a - part. How blue can you get, ba - by?

The an - swer's right here in my heart.

Verse

3. I gave you a brand new Ford, you said, "I wan-na Ca-dil-lac." I

bought you a ten dol-lar din-ner, you said, "Thanks for the snack." I

let you live in my pent-house, you said it was just a shack. I

gave ___ you ___ sev-en child ___ ren and ___ now ___ you ___ wan-na give 'em back. Yes, I've ___

been down-heart-ed ba - by, ev - er since

the day we met. _____ I say, ah, but

love is ___ noth-ing but the blues. ___ Ba - by,

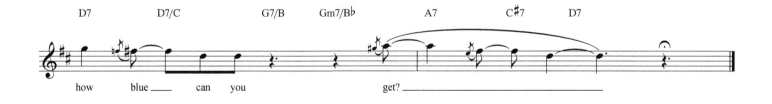

how blue ___ can you get? _____

Please Love Me

Words and Music by B.B. King and Jules Bihari

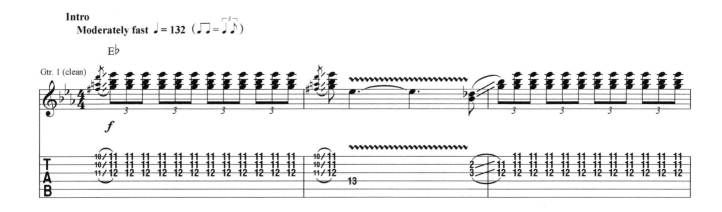

*Chord symbols reflect overall harmony.

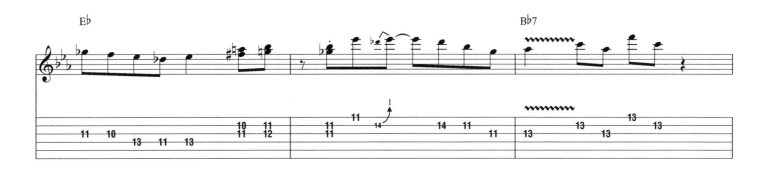

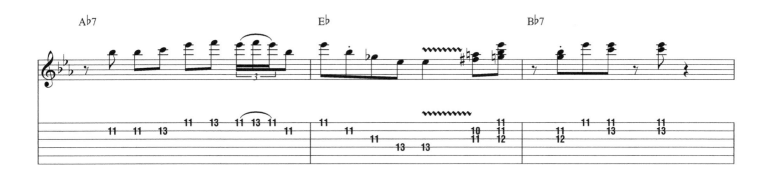

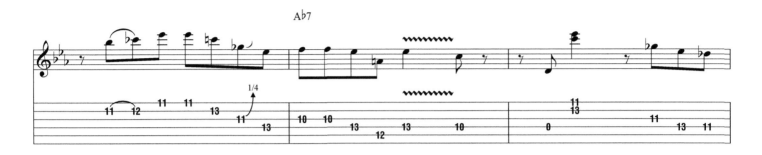

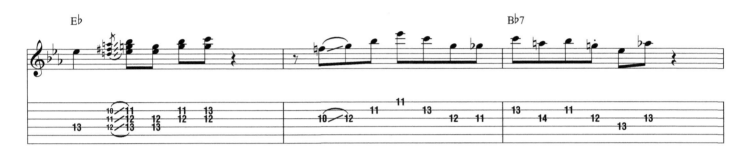

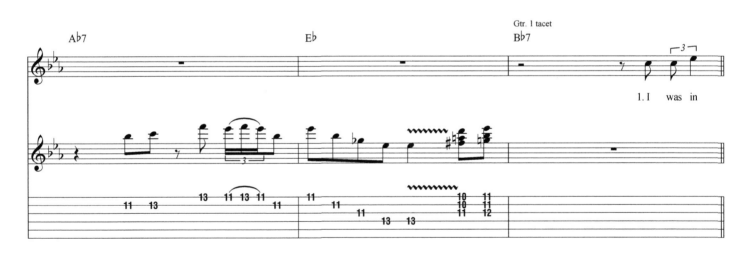

1. I was in

love with you,_ ba - by, hon-ey, be - fore_ I called_ your name. I was in

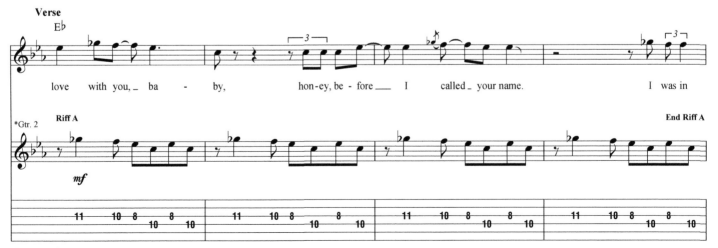

*Horns arr. for gtr.

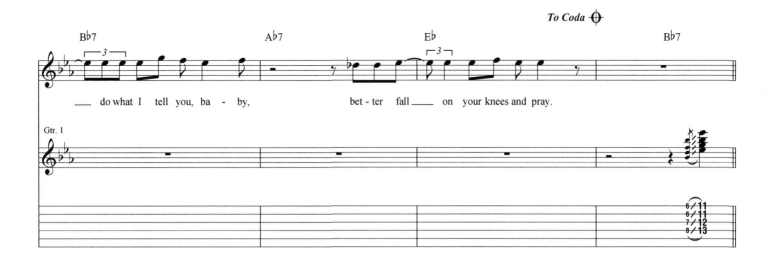

do what I tell you, ba - by,   bet - ter fall ____ on your knees and pray.

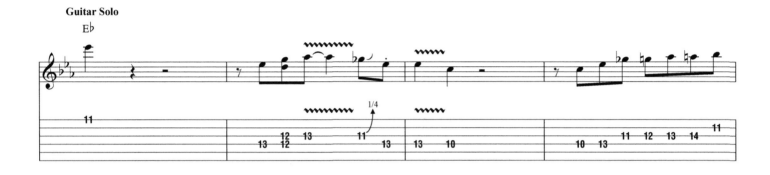

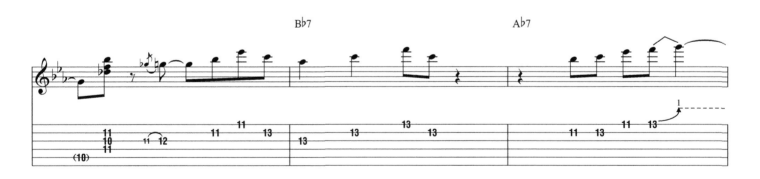

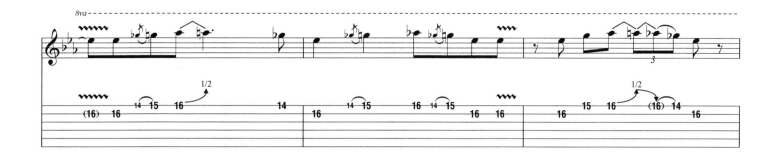

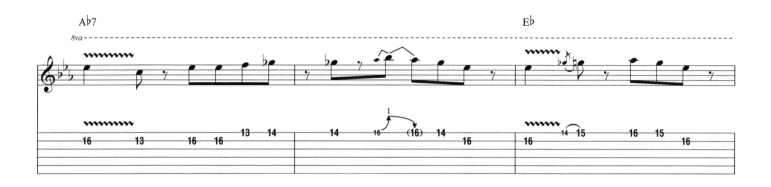

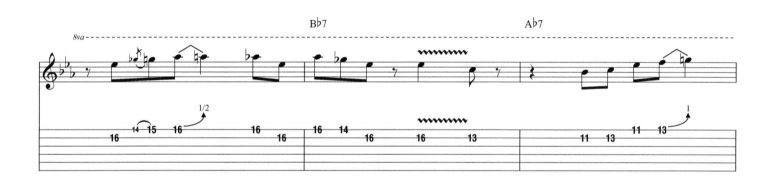

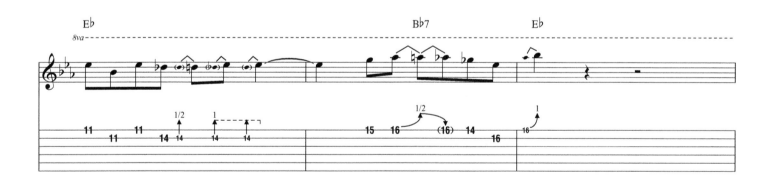

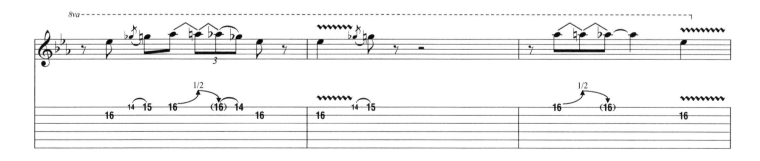

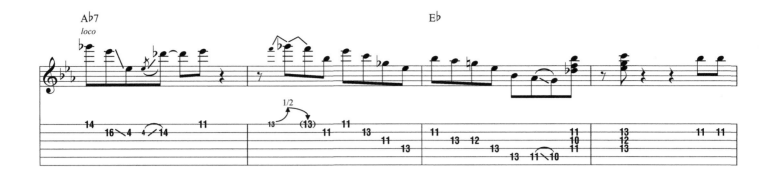

D.S. al Coda

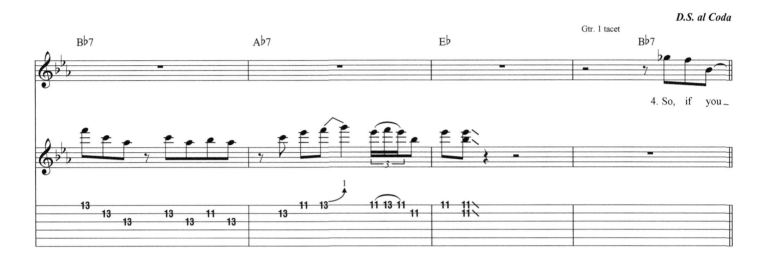

Gtr. 1 tacet

4. So, if you

Coda

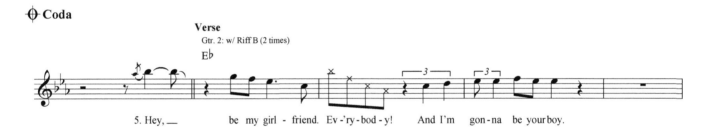

Verse
Gtr. 2: w/ Riff B (2 times)

5. Hey, ___ be my girl - friend. Ev - 'ry - bod - y! And I'm gon - na be your boy.

Want you to be my girl - friend, ba - by. Ba - by, I'm ___ gon-na be your boy. Gon - na buy a

___ Cad - il - lac car, ba - by, and find me wher - ev - er you ___ are. ___

Gtr. 2

let ring - - - - - - - - - - -

You Upset Me Baby

Words and Music by B.B. King and Jules Bihari

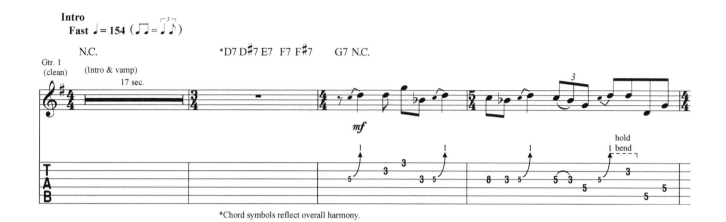

*Chord symbols reflect overall harmony.

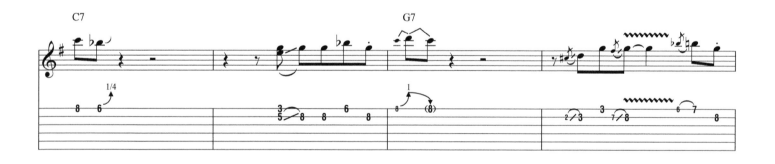

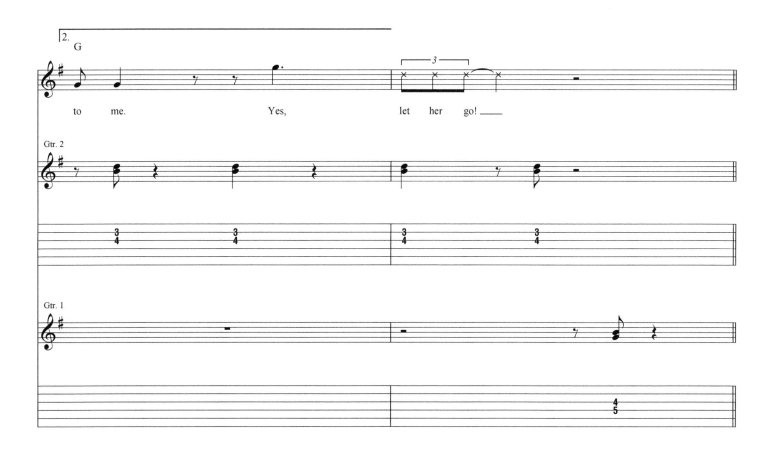

Saxophone Solo

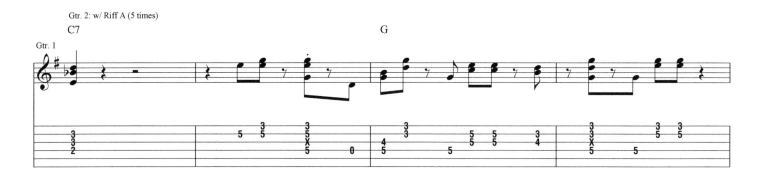

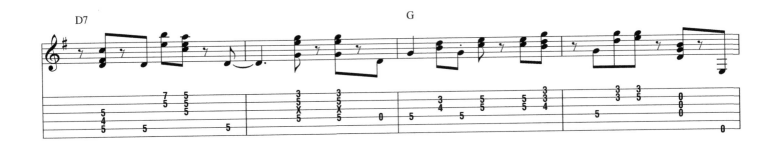

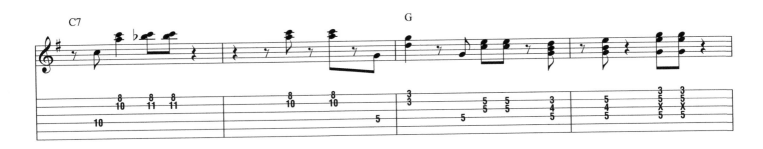

D.S. al Coda
(take 1st ending)

Gtr. 1 tacet

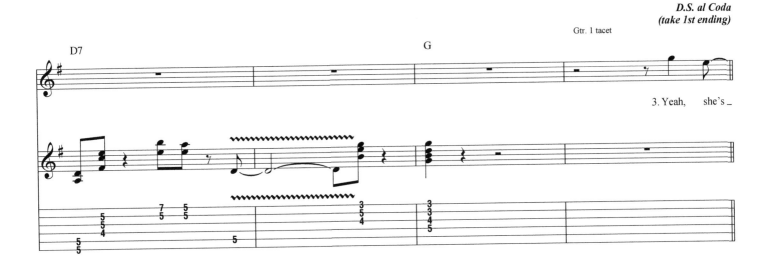

3. Yeah, she's

☩ **Coda**

be - in' hit by a ___ fal - len tree, wom - an, what you do to me. ___

28

Worry, Worry

Words and Music by Plumber Davis and Jules Bihari

Intro
Slow ♩. = 61

Spoken: Thank you so much.   Now, ladies and gentlemen,   we wanna go way back.

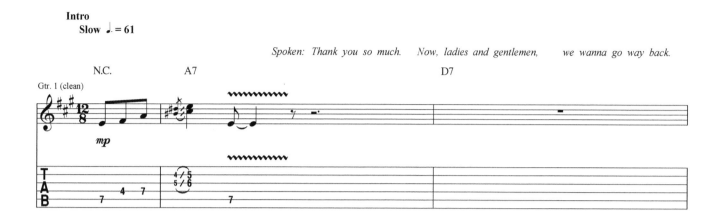

Way back.

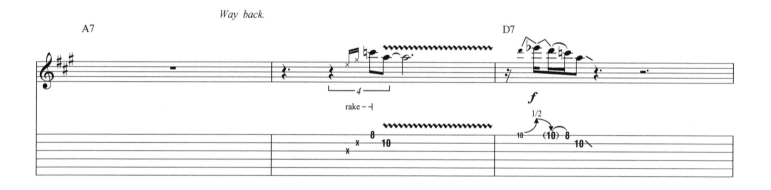

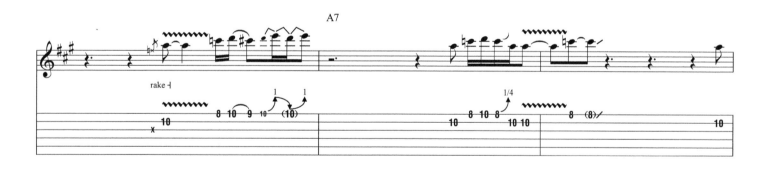

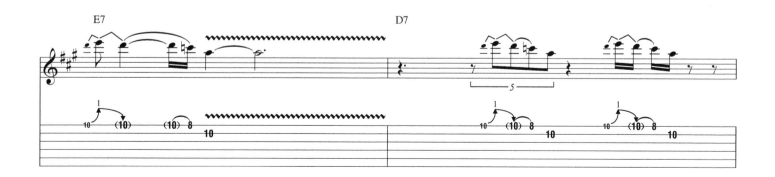

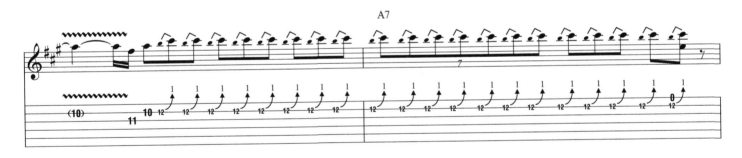

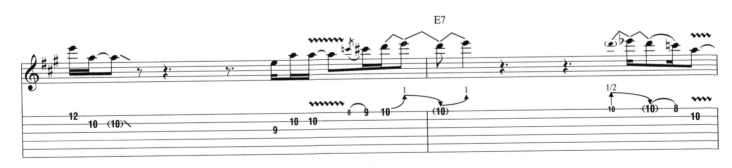

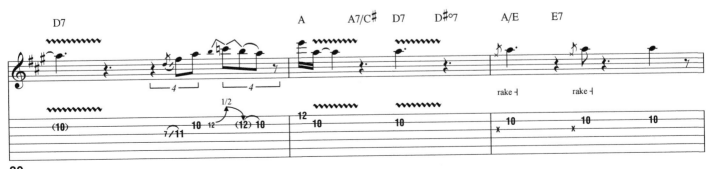

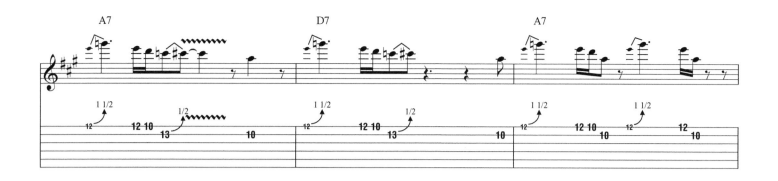

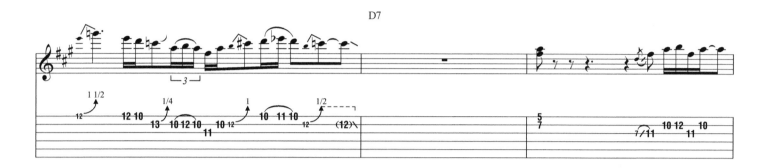

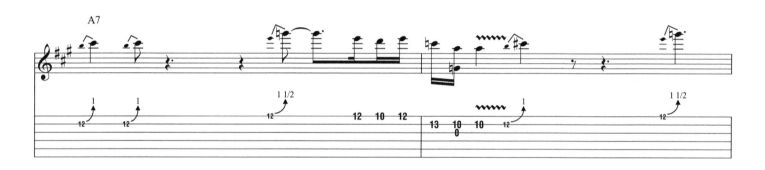

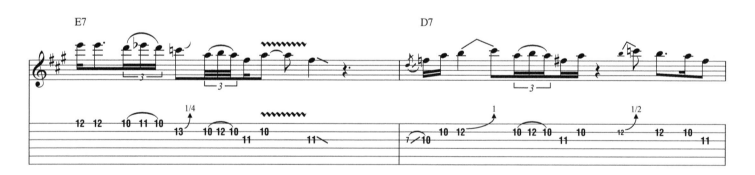

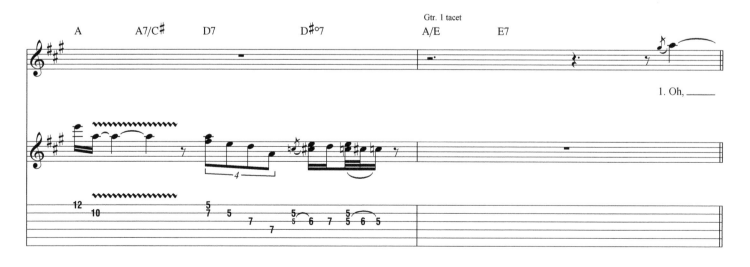

*Gtr. 2

*Horns arr. for gtr.

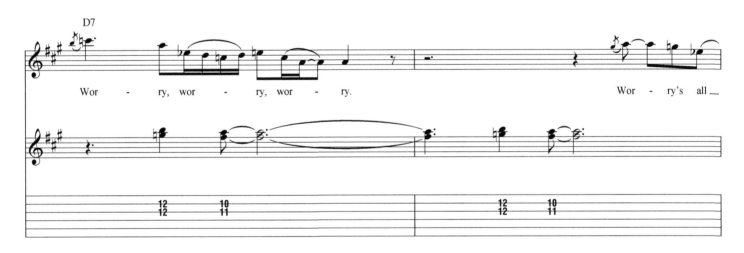

Interlude

Gtr. 2: w/ Riff A

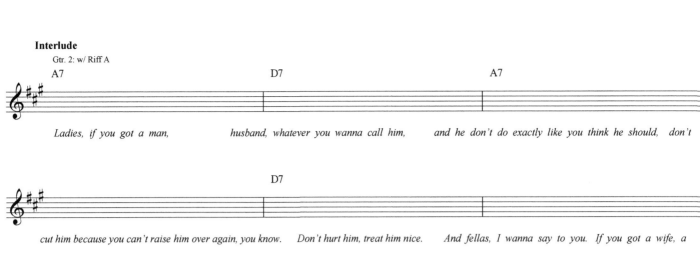

Ladies, if you got a man,   *husband, whatever you wanna call him,*   *and he don't do exactly like you think he should, don't*

cut him because you can't raise him over again, you know.   *Don't hurt him, treat him nice.*   *And fellas, I wanna say to you. If you got a wife, a*

woman or whatever you wanna call her, she don't do like you think she should, don't go upside her head.

That don't do but one thing: That make her a little smarter, and she won't let you catch her the next time.

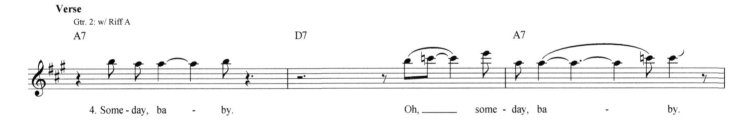

So all you do is talk to her softly, real sweet, you know.   *And you tell her, "I know you'll do better."*

Verse

Gtr. 2: w/ Riff A

4. Some-day, ba - by.   Oh, _____ some - day, ba - by.

Oh, _____ yes, _____ some - day, ba -

- by.   Oh, _____

___ yes, ___ some-day, babe, _ yeah!   5. Ah, ____

Verse

Gtr. 2: w/ Riff A (1st 10 meas.)

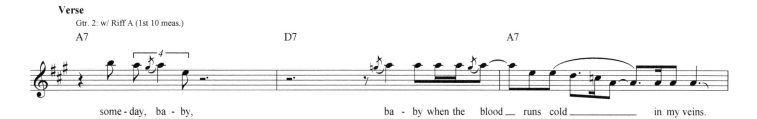

some - day, ba - by,   ba - by when the blood __ runs cold _____ in my veins.

Yes, __ some - day, babe,   ba - by when the blood

runs cold _____ in my veins. __   Yes, __ you won't

be ab - le to hurt old B no more _____ then, wom - an,   'cause __ my heart

won't _____ feel no pain. _____

Woke Up This Morning

Words and Music by B.B. King and Jules Bihari

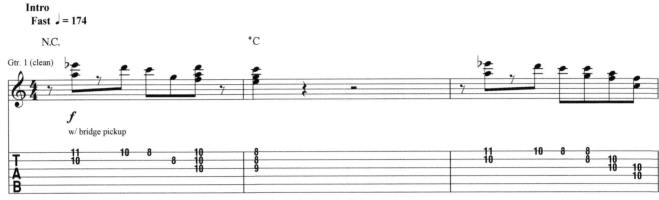

*Chord symbols reflect overall harmony.

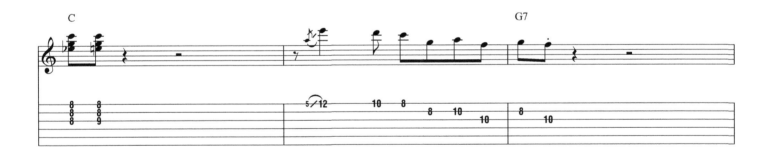

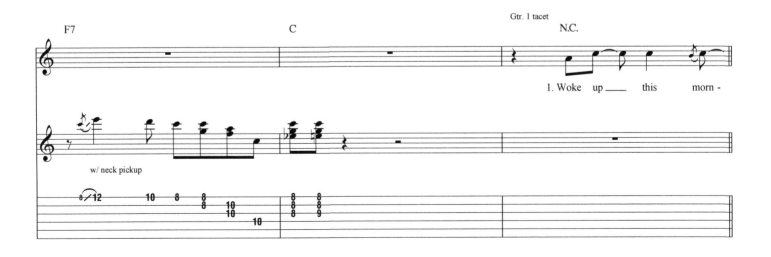

1. Woke up ___ this morn-

w/ neck pickup

Verse

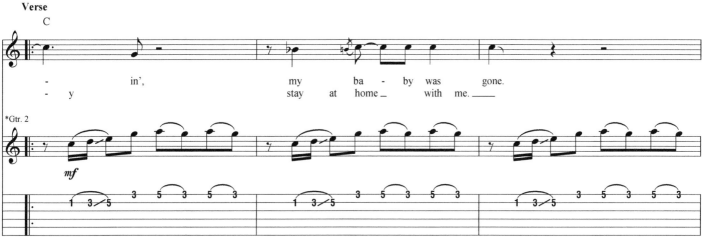

-in', my ba - by was gone.
-y stay at home __ with me. __

*Gtr. 2

*Horns arr. for gtr.

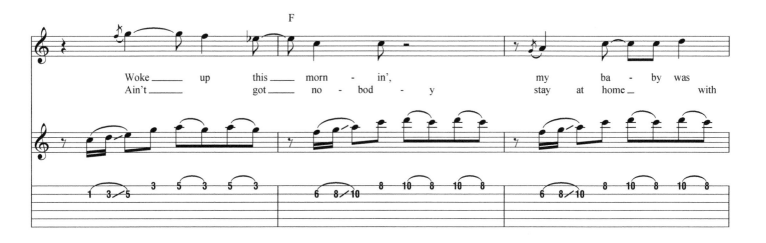

Woke __ up this __ morn - in', my ba - by was
Ain't __ got __ no - bod - y stay at home __ with

gone. I feel __ so __ bad __
me. My ba - by, she's __ gone. __

my ba - by's gone. __ 2. I ain't got no - bod - 3. I __ been __
I'm in mis - er - y.

You Done Lost Your Good Thing Now

Words and Music by B.B. King and Joe Bihari

Intro
Slow ♩ = 67

*Chord symbols reflect overall harmony.

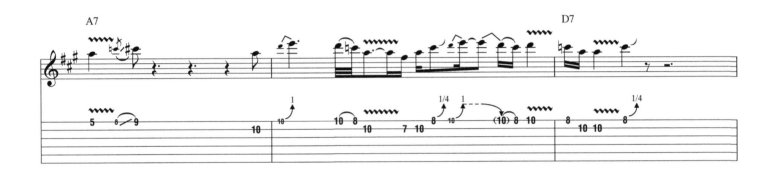

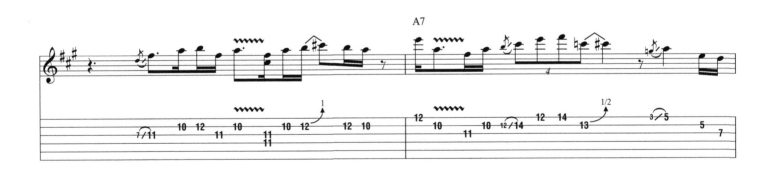

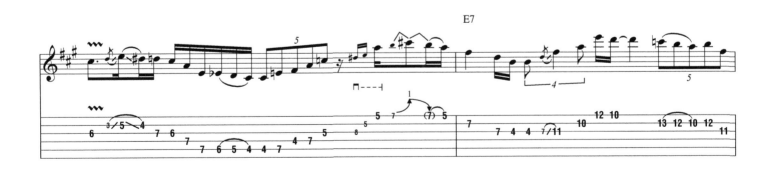

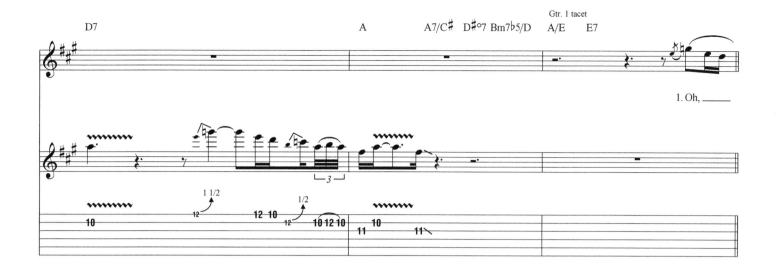

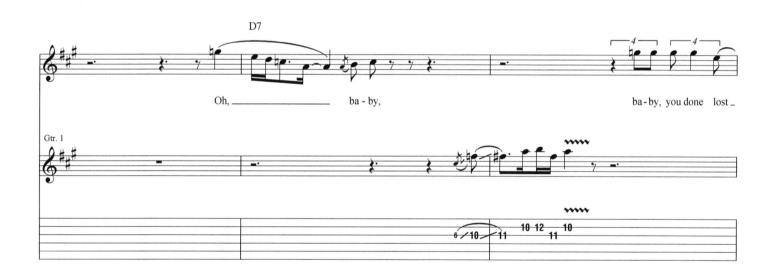

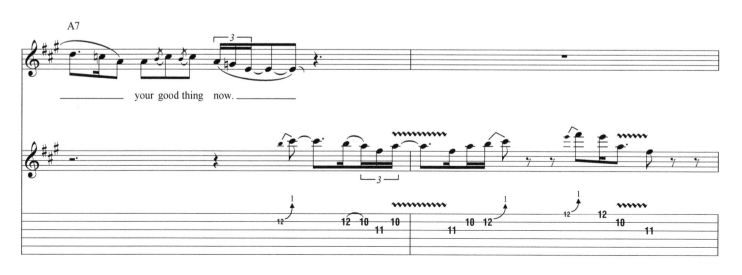

say that you love me, ba - by, and you would do

an - y - thing I said.

rake

But the way you treat me now, ba - by, ba - by, I would

much rath - er be dead.

rake

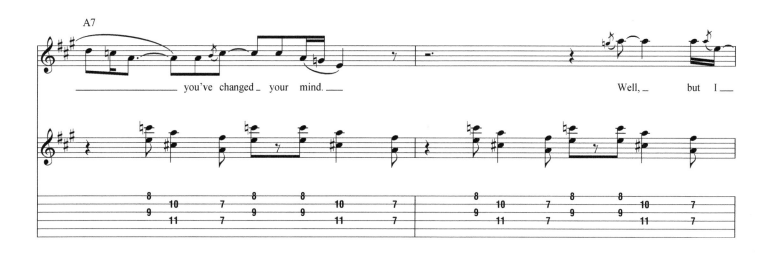

you've changed your mind. Well, but I

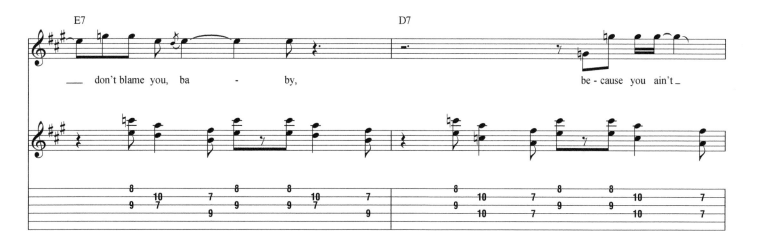

don't blame you, ba - by, be - cause you ain't

what you used to be. 4. Whoa would-n't let me, would-n't let me

End Riff A

Verse
Gtr. 2: w/ Riff A

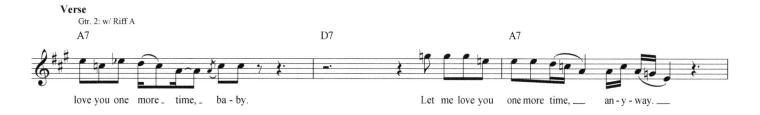

love you one more time, ba - by. Let me love you one more time, an - y - way.

Oh, ho, ho, ba - by, let me love you one

more time, ___ an-y-way. ___   Well, you know you can't quit me, now, ba - by,

be-cause you did-n't mean me no good ___ an-y-way.   5. Yeah, ___ yeah, ___

Verse
Gtr. 2: w/ Riff A (1st 11 meas.)

___ ba - by,   ba - by, you done lost ___ your good thing now. ___

Whoa, ___ ba - by,   you done lost ___ your good thing now.

___   Yes, ___ I say the way I used to,   the way I

used to love you, ba - by,   ba - by, that's the way ___ I hate you now. ___

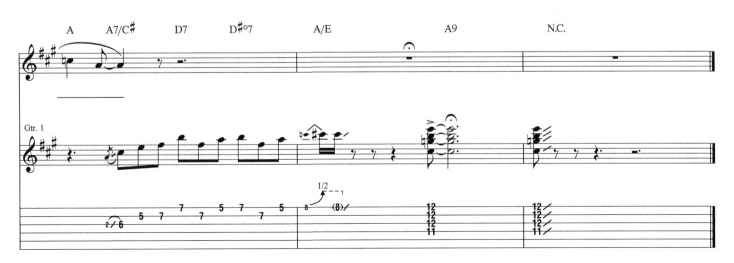

Help the Poor

Words and Music by Charlie Singleton

Drop D tuning:
(low to high) D-A-D-G-B-E

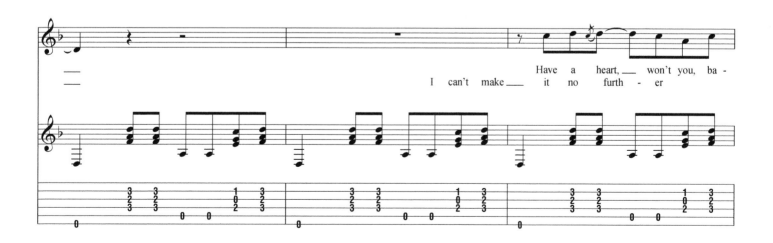

Outro

I'm in trou-ble, don't you see?　　　On-ly your love can

Gtr. 1: w/ Rhy. Fig. 2 (3 times)

save　me.　Help the poor,_____ help the poor.　　Help the poor,_____ help the

poor.　Help the poor,_____ help the poor.　　Help the poor,_____ help the

poor.　Help the poor,_____ help the poor.　　Help the poor,_____ help the

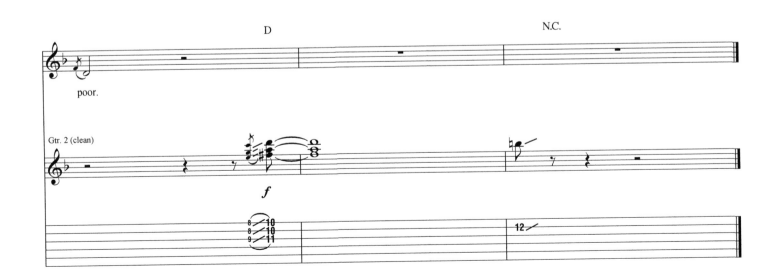

poor.

GUITAR NOTATION LEGEND

Guitar music can be notated three different ways: on a *musical staff*, in *tablature*, and in *rhythm slashes*.

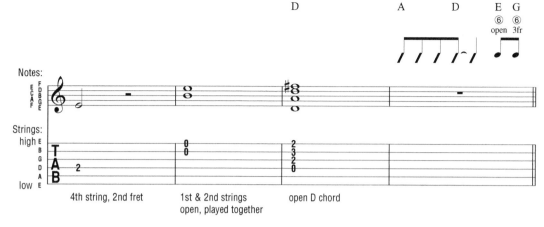

RHYTHM SLASHES are written above the staff. Strum chords in the rhythm indicated. Use the chord diagrams found at the top of the first page of the transcription for the appropriate chord voicings. Round noteheads indicate single notes.

THE MUSICAL STAFF shows pitches and rhythms and is divided by bar lines into measures. Pitches are named after the first seven letters of the alphabet.

TABLATURE graphically represents the guitar fingerboard. Each horizontal line represents a string, and each number represents a fret.

4th string, 2nd fret

1st & 2nd strings open, played together

open D chord

Definitions for Special Guitar Notation

HALF-STEP BEND: Strike the note and bend up 1/2 step.

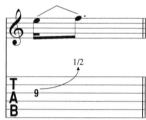

WHOLE-STEP BEND: Strike the note and bend up one step.

GRACE NOTE BEND: Strike the note and immediately bend up as indicated.

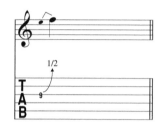

SLIGHT (MICROTONE) BEND: Strike the note and bend up 1/4 step.

BEND AND RELEASE: Strike the note and bend up as indicated, then release back to the original note. Only the first note is struck.

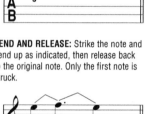

PRE-BEND: Bend the note as indicated, then strike it.

PRE-BEND AND RELEASE: Bend the note as indicated. Strike it and release the bend back to the original note.

UNISON BEND: Strike the two notes simultaneously and bend the lower note up to the pitch of the higher.

VIBRATO: The string is vibrated by rapidly bending and releasing the note with the fretting hand.

WIDE VIBRATO: The pitch is varied to a greater degree by vibrating with the fretting hand.

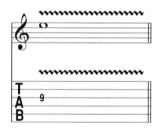

HAMMER-ON: Strike the first (lower) note with one finger, then sound the higher note (on the same string) with another finger by fretting it without picking.

PULL-OFF: Place both fingers on the notes to be sounded. Strike the first note and without picking, pull the finger off to sound the second (lower) note.

LEGATO SLIDE: Strike the first note and then slide the same fret-hand finger up or down to the second note. The second note is not struck.

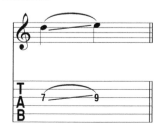

SHIFT SLIDE: Same as legato slide, except the second note is struck.

TRILL: Very rapidly alternate between the notes indicated by continuously hammering on and pulling off.

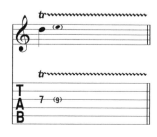

TAPPING: Hammer ("tap") the fret indicated with the pick-hand index or middle finger and pull off to the note fretted by the fret hand.

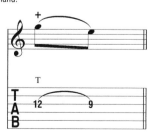

NATURAL HARMONIC: Strike the note while the fret-hand lightly touches the string directly over the fret indicated.

PINCH HARMONIC: The note is fretted normally and a harmonic is produced by adding the edge of the thumb or the tip of the index finger of the pick hand to the normal pick attack.

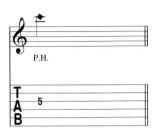

HARP HARMONIC: The note is fretted normally and a harmonic is produced by gently resting the pick hand's index finger directly above the indicated fret (in parentheses) while the pick hand's thumb or pick assists by plucking the appropriate string.

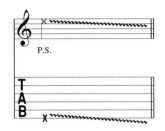

PICK SCRAPE: The edge of the pick is rubbed down (or up) the string, producing a scratchy sound.

MUFFLED STRINGS: A percussive sound is produced by laying the fret hand across the string(s) without depressing, and striking them with the pick hand.

PALM MUTING: The note is partially muted by the pick hand lightly touching the string(s) just before the bridge.

RAKE: Drag the pick across the strings indicated with a single motion.

TREMOLO PICKING: The note is picked as rapidly and continuously as possible.

ARPEGGIATE: Play the notes of the chord indicated by quickly rolling them from bottom to top.

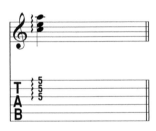

VIBRATO BAR DIVE AND RETURN: The pitch of the note or chord is dropped a specified number of steps (in rhythm), then returned to the original pitch.

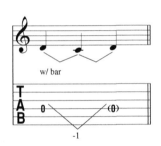

VIBRATO BAR SCOOP: Depress the bar just before striking the note, then quickly release the bar.

VIBRATO BAR DIP: Strike the note and then immediately drop a specified number of steps, then release back to the original pitch.

Additional Musical Definitions

(accent)	•	Accentuate note (play it louder).
(accent)	•	Accentuate note with great intensity.
(staccato)	•	Play the note short.
⊓	•	Downstroke
V	•	Upstroke

D.S. al Coda • Go back to the sign (𝄋), then play until the measure marked "*To Coda*," then skip to the section labelled "**Coda**."

D.C. al Fine • Go back to the beginning of the song and play until the measure marked "*Fine*" (end).

Rhy. Fig. • Label used to recall a recurring accompaniment pattern (usually chordal).

Riff • Label used to recall composed, melodic lines (usually single notes) which recur.

Fill • Label used to identify a brief melodic figure which is to be inserted into the arrangement.

Rhy. Fill • A chordal version of a Fill.

tacet • Instrument is silent (drops out).

• Repeat measures between signs.

• When a repeated section has different endings, play the first ending only the first time and the second ending only the second time.

NOTE: Tablature numbers in parentheses mean:
1. The note is being sustained over a system (note in standard notation is tied), or
2. The note is sustained, but a new articulation (such as a hammer-on, pull-off, slide or vibrato) begins, or
3. The note is a barely audible "ghost" note (note in standard notation is also in parentheses).

GUITAR RECORDED VERSIONS®

Guitar Recorded Versions® are note-for-note transcriptions of guitar music taken directly off recordings. This series, one of the most popular in print today, features some of the greatest guitar players and groups from blues and rock to country and jazz.

Guitar Recorded Versions are transcribed by the best transcribers in the business. Every book contains notes and tablature unless otherwise marked. Visit **halleonard.com** for our complete selection.

AUTHENTIC TRANSCRIPTIONS WITH NOTES AND TABLATURE

John 5
00690898 The Devil Knows
My Name $22.95
00690814 Songs for Sanity $19.95
00690751 Vertigo $19.95
Eric Johnson
00694912 Ah Via Musicom $24.99
00690660 Best of $29.99
00691076 Up Close $22.99
00690169 Venus Isle $29.99
Robert Johnson
00690271 New Transcriptions ... $27.99
Janis Joplin
00699131 Best of $24.99
Judas Priest
00690427 Best of $24.99
Kansas
00690277 Best of $24.99
Phil Keaggy
00690911 Best of $24.99
Toby Keith
00690727 Guitar Collection $19.99
The Killers
00690910 Sam's Town $19.95
Killswitch Engage
00120814 Disarm the Descent ... $22.99
Albert King
00690504 Very Best of $24.99
00124869 In Session $24.99
B.B. King
00690492 Anthology $29.99
00130447 Live at the Regal $19.99
00690444 Riding with the King .. $24.99
Freddie King
00690134 Collection $22.99
Marcus King
00327968 El Dorado $22.99
Kiss
00690157 Alive! $19.99
00690356 Alive II $24.99
00694903 Best of $29.99
00690355 Destroyer $19.99
00291163 Very Best of $24.99
Mark Knopfler
00690164 Guitar Styles $27.99
Greg Koch
00345767 Best of $29.99
Korn
00690780 Greatest Hits Vol. 1 .... $24.99
Kris Kristofferson
00690377 Collection $22.99
Lamb of God
00690834 Ashes of the Wake $24.99
00691187 Resolution $22.99
00690875 Sacrament $24.99
Ray LaMontagne
00690977 Gossip in the Grain ... $19.99
00691057 God Willin' & The
Creek Don't Rise $22.99
John Lennon
00690679 Guitar Collection $27.99
Linkin Park
00690922 Minutes to Midnight .. $22.99
The Lumineers
00114563 The Lumineers $22.99
George Lynch
00690525 Best of $29.99
Lynyrd Skynyrd
00690955 All-Time Greatest Hits. $24.99
00694954 New Best of $24.99
Yngwie Malmsteen
00690577 Anthology $29.99
Marilyn Manson
00690754 Lest We Forget $22.99
Bob Marley
00694956 Legend $22.99
00694945 Songs of Freedom $29.99
Pat Martino
00139168 Guitar Anthology $29.99
John McLaughlin
00129105 Guitar Tab Anthology .. $27.99
Mastodon
00690989 Crack the Skye $24.99
00236690 Emperor of Sand $22.99

00691176 The Hunter $24.99
00137718 Once More 'Round
the Sun $24.99
Andy McKee
00691942 Art of Motion $24.99
00691034 Joyland $19.99
Don McLean
00120080 Songbook $22.99
Megadeth
00694952 Countdown to
Extinction $24.99
00691015 Endgame $27.99
00276065 Greatest Hits $27.99
00694951 Rust in Peace $27.99
00690011 Youthanasia $24.99
John Mellencamp
00690505 Guitar Collection $24.99
Metallica
00209876 Hardwired...
To Self-Destruct $24.99
Pat Metheny
00690562 Bright Size Life $24.99
00691073 Day Trip/
Tokyo Day Trip Live ... $22.99
00690646 One Quiet Night $24.99
00690559 Question & Answer $27.99
00690558 Trio 99-00 .... $24.99
00690561 Trio Live $27.99
00118836 Unity Band $22.99
00102590 What's It All About $24.99
Steve Miller Band
00690040 Young Hearts: Complete
Greatest Hits $24.99
Ministry
00119338 Guitar Tab Collection .. $24.99
Wes Montgomery
00102591 Guitar Anthology $27.99
Gary Moore
00691092 Best of $27.99
00694802 Still Got the Blues $24.99
Alanis Morissette
00355456 Jagged Little Pill $22.99
Motion City Soundtrack
00691005 Best of $19.99
Mountain
00694958 Best of $22.99
Mumford & Sons
00691070 Sigh No More $22.99
Muse
00118196 The 2nd Law $19.99
00151195 Drones $19.99
My Morning Jacket
00690996 Collection $19.99
Matt Nathanson
00690984 Some Mad Hope $22.99
Night Ranger
00690883 Best of $19.99
Nirvana
00690611 Nirvana $24.99
00694895 Bleach $22.99
00694913 In Utero $22.99
00694883 Nevermind $19.99
00690026 Unplugged
in New York $19.99
Nothing More
00265439 Guitar & Bass Tab
Collection $24.99
The Offspring
00690807 Greatest Hits $24.99
Opeth
00243349 Best of $22.99
Roy Orbison
00691052 Black & White Night .. $22.99
Ozzy Osbourne
00694847 Best of $27.99
Brad Paisley
00690933 Best of $27.99
00690995 Play $29.99
Christopher Parkening
00690939 Solo Pieces $24.99
Les Paul
00690594 Best of $24.99
Pearl Jam
00694855 Ten $24.99
Periphery
00146043 Guitar Tab Collection .. $24.99

Carl Perkins
00690725 Best of $19.99
Tom Petty
00690499 Definitive Collection .. $24.99
Phish
00690176 Billy Breathes $24.99
Pink Floyd
00121933 Acoustic Collection ... $27.99
00690428 Dark Side of
the Moon $22.99
00142677 The Endless River $19.99
00244637 Guitar Anthology $24.99
00239799 The Wall $27.99
Poison
00690789 Best of $22.99
Elvis Presley
00690299 King of Rock 'n' Roll . $22.99
Prince
00690925 Very Best of $24.99
Queen
00690003 Classic Queen $24.99
00694975 Greatest Hits $27.99
Queens of the Stone Age
00254332 Villains $22.99
Queensryche
00690670 Very Best of $27.99
The Raconteurs
00690878 Broken Boy Soldiers ... $19.95
Radiohead
00109303 Guitar Anthology $29.99
Rage Against the Machine
00694910 Rage Against the
Machine $24.99
00119834 Guitar Anthology $24.99
Rancid
00690179 And Out Come the
Wolves $24.99
Ratt
00690426 Best of $24.99
Red Hot Chili Peppers
00690055 BloodSugarSexMagik .. $19.99
00690584 By the Way $24.99
00690379 Californication $22.99
00182634 The Getaway $24.99
00690673 Greatest Hits $24.99
00691166 I'm with You $22.99
00690255 Mother's Milk $24.99
00690090 One Hot Minute $22.95
00690852 Stadium Arcadium $29.99
00706518 Unlimited Loved $27.99
Jerry Reed
00694892 Guitar Style of $24.99
Django Reinhardt
00690511 Definitive Collection .. $24.99
Jimmie Rodgers
00690260 Guitar Collection $22.99
Rolling Stones
00690014 Exile on Main Street .. $24.99
00690631 Guitar Anthology $34.99
00694976 Some Girls $22.95
00690264 Tattoo You $19.95
Angelo Romero
00690974 Bella $19.99
David Lee Roth
00690685 Eat 'Em and Smile $24.99
00690942 Songs of Van Halen ... $19.95
Rush
00323854 The Spirit of Radio $22.99
Santana
00173534 Guitar Anthology $29.99
00690031 Greatest Hits $24.99
Joe Satriani
00276350 What Happens Next ... $24.99
Michael Schenker
00690796 Very Best of $24.99
Matt Schofield
00128870 Guitar Tab Collection .. $22.99
Scorpions
00690566 Best of $24.99
Bob Seger
00690604 Guitar Collection $24.99
Ed Sheeran
00234543 Divide $22.99
00138870 X $19.99

Kenny Wayne Shepherd
00690803 Best of $24.99
00151178 Ledbetter Heights $19.99
Shinedown
00692433 Amaryllis $22.99
Skillet
00122218 Rise $22.99
Slash
00691114 Guitar Anthology $34.99
Slayer
00690872 Christ Illusion $19.95
00690813 Guitar Collection $24.99
Slipknot
00690419 Slipknot $22.99
00690973 All Hope Is Gone $24.99
Smashing Pumpkins
00316982 Greatest Hits $24.99
Social Distortion
00690330 Live at the Roxy $24.99
Soundgarden
00690912 Guitar Anthology $24.99
Steely Dan
00120004 Best of $27.99
Steppenwolf
00694921 Best of $22.95
Mike Stern
00690655 Best of $27.99
Cat Stevens
14041588 Tea for the Tillerman .. $19.99
Rod Stewart
00690949 Guitar Anthology $19.99
Stone Temple Pilots
00322564 Thank You $26.99
Styx
00690520 Guitar Collection $22.99
Sublime
00120081 Sublime $22.99
00120122 40 oz. to Freedom $24.99
00690992 Robbin' the Hood $19.99
SUM 41
00690519 All Killer No Filler $19.95
00690929 Underclass Hero $19.95
Supertramp
00691072 Best of $24.99
Taylor Swift
00690994 Taylor Swift $22.99
00690993 Fearless $22.99
00115957 Red $21.99
00691063 Speak Now $22.99
System of a Down
00690531 Toxicity $19.99
James Taylor
00694824 Best of $22.99
Thin Lizzy
00694887 Best of $22.99
.38 Special
00690988 Guitar Anthology $22.99
Three Days Grace
00691039 Life Starts Now $22.99
Trans-Siberian Orchestra
00150209 Guitar Anthology $19.99
Merle Travis
00690233 Collection $24.99
Trivium
00253237 Guitar Tab Anthology .. $24.99
00123862 Vengeance Falls $24.99
Robin Trower
00690683 Bridge of Sighs $19.99
U2
00699191 Best of: 1980-1990 ... $24.99
00690732 Best of: 1990-2000 ... $29.99
00690894 18 Singles $27.99

Keith Urban
00124461 Guitar Anthology $29.99
Steve Vai
00690039 Alien Love Secrets $24.99
00690575 Alive in an
Ultra World $22.95
00690172 Fire Garden $34.99
00156024 Guitar Anthology $39.99
00197570 Modern Primitive $29.99
00660137 Passion & Warfare $29.99
00690881 Real Illusions:
Reflections $27.99
00690605 The Elusive Light
and Sound, Vol. 1 ..... $29.99
00694904 Sex and Religion $24.95
00110385 The Story of Light $24.99
00690392 The Ultra Zone $19.95
Van Halen
00700555 Van Halen $22.99
00295076 30 Classics $29.99
00700092 1984 .... $24.99
00700558 Fair Warning $24.99
Stevie Ray Vaughan
00690024 Couldn't Stand
the Weather $22.99
00690116 Guitar Collection $29.99
00694879 In the Beginning $19.95
00660136 In Step $24.99
00660058 Lightnin' Blues 83-87 . $29.99
00690550 Live at Montreux $29.99
00217455 Plays Slow Blues $24.99
00694835 The Sky Is Crying $24.99
00690025 Soul to Soul $19.95
00690015 Texas Flood $22.99
Volbeat
00109770 Guitar Collection $24.99
00121808 Outlaw Gentlemen
& Shady Ladies $24.99
T-Bone Walker
00690132 Collection $22.99
Muddy Waters
00694789 Deep Blues $27.99
Doc Watson
00152161 Guitar Anthology $24.99
Weezer
00690071 The Blue Album $22.99
00691046 Rarities Edition $22.99
Paul Westerberg & The Replacements
00691036 Very Best of $19.99
The White Stripes
00237811 Greatest Hits $24.99
Whitesnake
00117511 Guitar Collection $24.99
The Who
00691941 Acoustic Guitar
Collection $22.99
00690447 Best of $24.99
Wilco
00691006 Guitar Collection $24.99
The Yardbirds
00690596 Best of $24.99
Yes
00122303 Guitar Collection $24.99
Dwight Yoakam
00690916 Best of $22.99
Frank Zappa
00690507 Apostrophe $22.99
00690443 Hot Rats $22.99
00690624 One Size Fits All $27.99
00690623 Over-Nite Sensation .. $24.99
ZZ Top
00121684 Early Classics $27.99
00690589 Guitar Anthology $27.99
00690960 Guitar Classics $24.99

Complete songlists and more at **www.halleonard.com**
Prices and availability subject to change without notice.